MUSCLE CARS

by Jeffrey Zuehlke

Jan Lahtonen, consultant and safety engineer, auto mechanic, and a
member of the Porsche Club of America and the Audi Club of America

Lerner Publications Company • Minneapolis

For Dad

Cover Photo: Power and style were hallmarks of the 1970 Pontiac GTO Judge.

A Word about Measurement Conversions
To preserve authenticity, the original U.S. standard units of measure used for vintage car engines
have not been converted to their metric equivalents. For the same reason, the metric measures used
for modern car engines have not been converted to their U.S. standard measurements. A handy metric
conversion tool can found at http://www.csgnetwork.com/cubicinchlitercvt.html.

Lerner Publications Company
A division of Lerner Publishing Group
241 First Avenue North
Minneapolis, MN 55401 U.S.A.

Website address: www.lernerbooks.com

Library of Congress Cataloging-in-Publication Data

Zuehlke, Jeffrey, 1968–
    Muscle cars / by Jeffrey Zuehlke.
      p.   cm. — (Motor mania)
    Includes bibliographical references and index.
    ISBN-13: 978–0–8225–5927–6 (lib. bdg. : alk. paper)
    ISBN-10: 0–8225–5927–7 (lib. bdg. : alk. paper)
    1. Muscle cars—Juvenile literature.   I. Title.   II. Series.
  TL147.Z84 2007
  629.222—dc22   2005032495

Manufactured in the United States of America
1 2 3 4 5 6 – DP – 12 11 10 09 08 07

Contents

WHAT IS A MUSCLE CAR?

What is a muscle car? Some people say it's any car with "muscle"—a big, strong engine that can power the car to very high speeds. But many people have a more specific idea of what makes a muscle car. For them, muscle cars are a group of cars built in the United States from about 1964 to about 1972. Most of the cars were midsized and affordable.

This period was an exciting time in U.S. car history. U.S. automakers were creating some of the fastest and most powerful cars ever built. Those years were all about high performance and horsepower. High-performance cars are built to perform well at high speeds. Horsepower is the measure of an engine's power—how fast the engine can make the car go. The muscle car years produced many of the greatest cars of all time. These amazing machines include the Pontiac GTO, the Oldsmobile 4-4-2, the Chevrolet Chevelle SS, the Plymouth Road Runner, the Dodge Charger, and the Ford Cobra Jet Mustang.

These lightning-fast cars are still highly prized collectors items. Muscle car owners show off their machines at car shows around the country. And fans travel far and wide to admire these machines. Muscle cars are an important part of U.S. car history.

A customized 1968 Chevrolet Camaro burns rubber as it jumps off the starting line during a drag race. Power and speed are what muscle cars are all about.

Chapter One

MUSCLE CAR HISTORY

Restored Ford Model Ts from the early 1900s

oing fast—whether on a powerful horse or in a powerful machine—is exciting. So when the automobile was invented in the late 1800s, people nat-urally wanted to see how fast the new "horseless carriages" could go.

But those early machines didn't ex-actly burn rubber. Most cars of the early 1900s had big, inefficient engines that only produced about 5 horse-power. (Modern road cars produce about 150 horsepower.) Few could go much faster than 20 miles (32 kilome-ters) per hour.

Speed Sells

Henry Ford, founder of the Ford Motor Company, was an early U.S. automaker.

He raced his cars to make a name for himself and his company. In 1902 Ford mounted a massive engine onto a simple car frame. He called his new race car the *999*, after a famous train of the time. The following year, driver Barney Oldfield reached the amazing speed of 60 miles (95 km) per hour in the *999*. But most cars of the time couldn't go nearly that fast.

As time passed, auto builders kept improving their cars. They made them bigger, sturdier, and more dependable. The cars were also faster. Automakers developed better engines. These engines could produce not just a little horsepower but hundreds of horsepower. Automakers showed off their latest models on the racetrack.

Henry Ford *(right)*, Barney Oldfield, and the *999* racer. The car's gigantic engine made such a fearsome sound that Ford would not drive it on the streets.

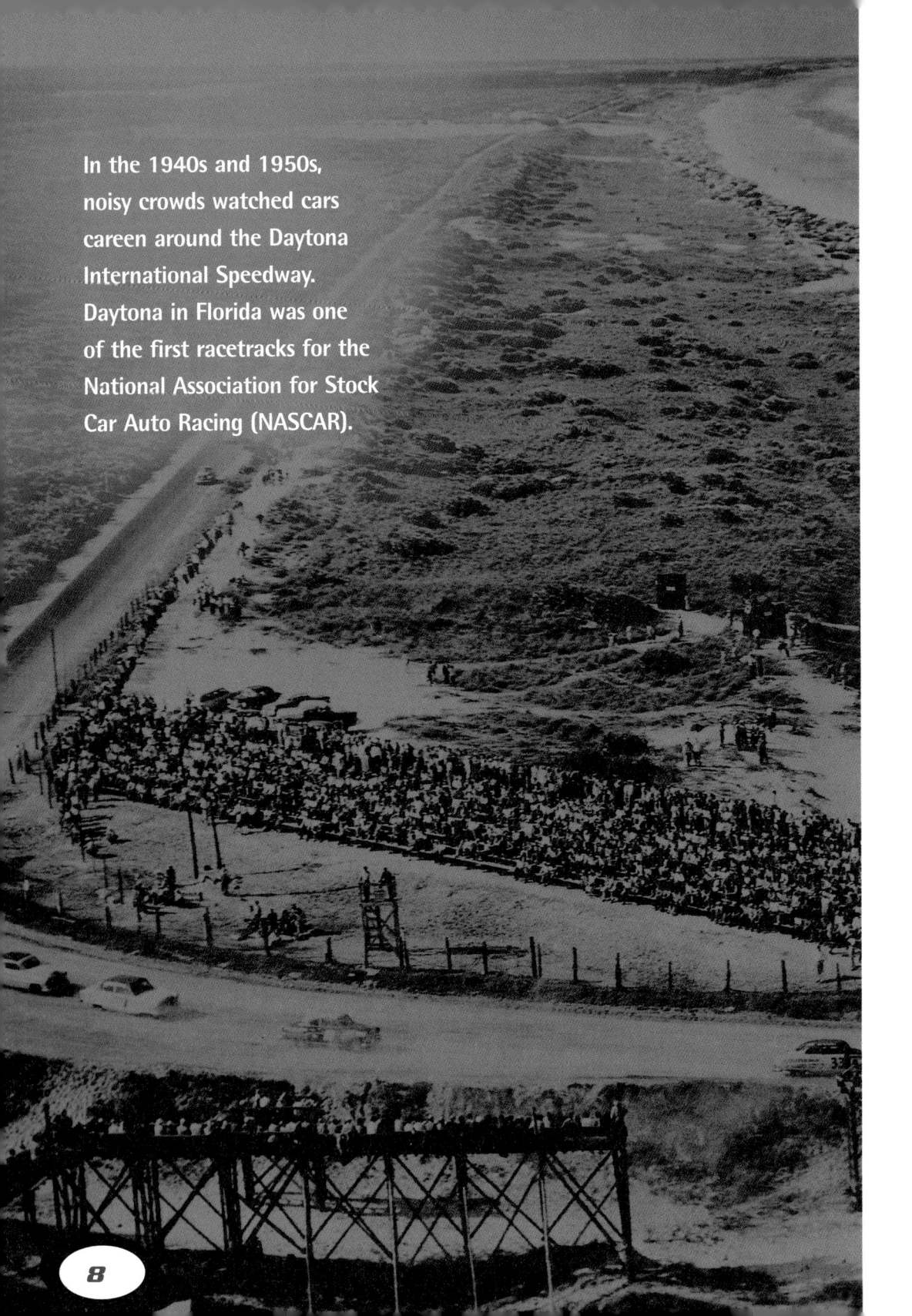

In the 1940s and 1950s, noisy crowds watched cars careen around the Daytona International Speedway. Daytona in Florida was one of the first racetracks for the National Association for Stock Car Auto Racing (NASCAR).

Early Muscle Cars

Ask some people when the muscle car was invented, and they'll tell you 1936. That was the year Buick stuffed a massive eight-cylinder engine into a mid-sized Buick Special body. The company called its new car the Century. This powerful machine immediately became one of the fastest cars on the road. It had a 320-cubic-inch engine that could produce 120 horsepower. It also stole the show on racetracks around the country.

Another muscle car milestone was passed 13 years later. In 1949 Oldsmobile introduced the Rocket 88. It was equipped with a 303-cubic-inch engine that produced 135 horsepower. The Rocket 88 really soared. It zoomed past most of the competition during the early days of a new racing league. The new group was the National Association for Stock Car Auto Racing.

As the 1940s rolled into the 1950s, NASCAR grew in popularity. U.S. car

The 1955 C-300 had a huge engine and lots of style. But some muscle car fans think it was too big to be a true muscle car.

engines changed too. Automakers were constantly trying to outdo one another on the track. So they made speed a high priority in the 1950s. One of the fastest cars of the time was the Chrysler 300 letter series. The C-300 was the first model in this series. It appeared during the 1955 model year. The C-300 featured the most powerful engine—the 331-cubic-inch Hemi V8—that was mass produced (made in large numbers). The 300 stood for the amount of horsepower the car's engine produced.

The letter series cars brought Chrysler win after win on NASCAR tracks in the late 1950s. But was the C-300 a true muscle car? The C-300 was a big, roomy, expensive car. Some people say a true muscle car is a small or midsized car. For that reason, many people don't count the letter series vehicles as true muscle cars.

Engine Sizes

The size of an automobile engine is measured as displacement. Engine displacement is the total volume (total room) of all cylinders. Before and during the muscle car era, displacement was measured in cubic inches in the United States. Automakers changed to cubic centimeters or liters in the 1970s.

DID YOU KNOW?

Henry Ford founded the Ford Motor Company in Dearborn, Michigan, on June 16, 1903. By the 1910s, Ford had become the world's largest automaker.

How an Internal Combustion Engine Works

Internal combustion engines create power by burning a mixture of fuel and air *(right)*. What makes muscle car engines special are their size and power. Nearly all muscle car engines are V8s. Most small or midsized cars have four- or six-cylinder engines that produce less horsepower—between 100 to 200 horsepower. But a big V8 can produce 300, 400, or more horsepower. More horsepower means more speed.

V8 ENGINE

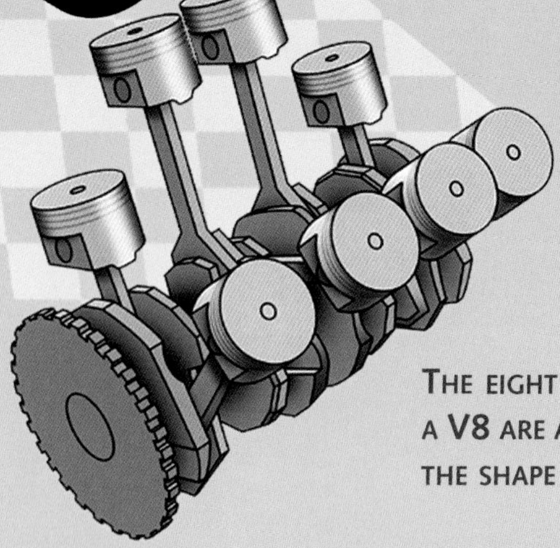

THE EIGHT PISTONS ON A **V8** ARE ARRANGED IN THE SHAPE OF A **V**.

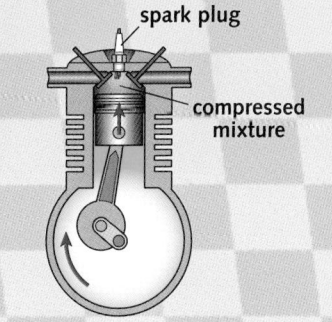

1. INTAKE STROKE
The piston moves down the cylinder and draws the fuel-air mixture into the cylinder through the intake valve.

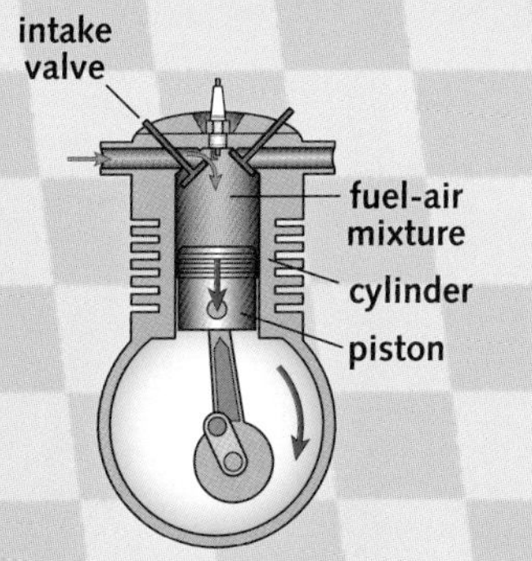

intake valve

fuel-air mixture

cylinder

piston

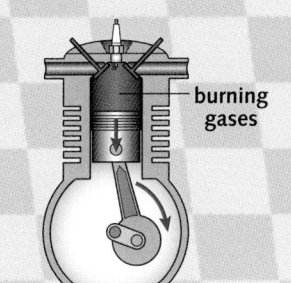

2. COMPRESSION STROKE
The piston moves up and compresses the fuel-air mixture. The spark plug ignites the mixture, creating combustion (burning).

spark plug

compressed mixture

3. POWER STROKE
The burning gases created by combustion push the piston downward. This gives the engine its power.

burning gases

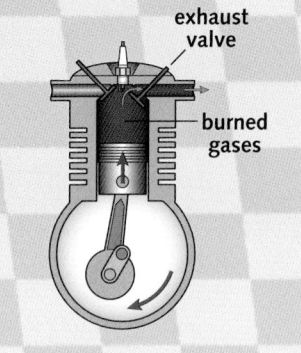

4. EXHAUST STROKE
The piston moves up again and pushes out the burned-out exhaust gases through the exhaust valve.

exhaust valve

burned gases

Boomers and the Muscle Car Boom

By the early 1960s, U.S. automakers continued to offer a handful of high-performance models. They included Chevrolet's 1961 Impala Super Sport (SS) 409. But these cars were not built or sold in large numbers. Automakers didn't believe many people wanted to buy fast cars.

Yet, at this very same time, a whole new generation of young people was reaching driving age. The U.S. baby boomers were the result of a huge rise in births after World War II (1939–1945).

Measuring Performance

Top speed and acceleration are the two most popular ways to measure a car's performance. A car's top speed is how fast it can go. Acceleration is how fast a car can get going from a standing stop. Acceleration is usually measured in two ways. One is how fast the car can go from 0 to 60 miles (0 to 97 km) per hour. The other is how fast the car can cover a quarter mile (0.40 km) from a standing start.

The baby boomers (1946–1964) were the largest generation in U.S. history.

The Chevrolet Impala SS—named after a speedy African antelope—gave people a new idea of what a high-performance car could be.

Baby boomers showed up at wide dirt tracks to watch hot rod races. Their interest told automakers that boomers wanted cool, fast cars.

They were also the richest. The U.S. economy had done well in the years after the war. Many young people could afford to buy new cars. And, of course, they wanted fast, cool cars.

Hot-rodding—fixing up old cars for racing—was very popular with teenagers at the time. Even rock musicians were writing songs about cool cars. One of the biggest hits of 1962 was "409" by the Beach Boys. This was a song about a speedy Chevy Impala SS 409. Similar hits followed. The car craze was picking up speed.

Mustangs and Goats

The auto industry saw what was going on. Lee Iacocca, general manager of Ford, led the charge to develop the Ford Mustang. The Mustang had just about everything a young driver could want. It was sleek, sporty, and affordable. The Mustang was hugely popular when it was introduced in April 1964.

But the Mustang was missing one thing—speed.

Around this same time, officials at Pontiac were cooking up their own hot car. Engineer John DeLorean and his team put a powerful V8 engine into a midsized Pontiac Tempest.

The result was the 1964 Pontiac Tempest GTO. It was the world's first true muscle car. With its smooth lines, the GTO had the kind of look young people wanted. But looks weren't the only cool thing about it. The GTO was equipped with a 389-cubic-inch V8 engine that produced almost 350 horsepower. It was one of the fastest cars on the market. And best of all for young car buyers, the GTO was affordable. It sold for less than $3,500 (about $20,000 in modern times).

Nicknamed the Goat, the GTO was an instant hit. Pontiac sold tens of thousands of them in 1964.

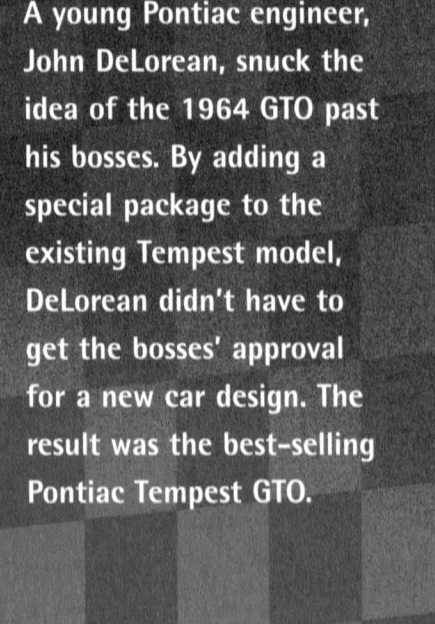

DID YOU KNOW?

Ford actually named its Mustang after a World War II fighter plane. Car fans thought the name came from the untamed mustang horses that live in the wild. Either way, Ford saw the name as the perfect choice for its exciting new car.

A young Pontiac engineer, John DeLorean, snuck the idea of the 1964 GTO past his bosses. By adding a special package to the existing Tempest model, DeLorean didn't have to get the bosses' approval for a new car design. The result was the best-selling Pontiac Tempest GTO.

That Thing Got a Hemi?

In a typical muscle car engine, the air and fuel mixture is drawn into the combustion chamber. The upward movement of the piston presses together the air and fuel mixture. Then a spark plug ignites (sets fire) to the mixture, pushing the piston downward and creating power.

Hemi is a nickname for a special kind of engine made popular by the Chrysler Corporation. *Hemi* is short for hemispherical, or half spherical. The Hemi engine gets its name from its special hemispherical combustion chambers. A Hemi's half-spherical chambers burn fuel more efficiently than most engine designs. The efficient design makes for more horsepower and usually more speed.

Hemi Cylinder

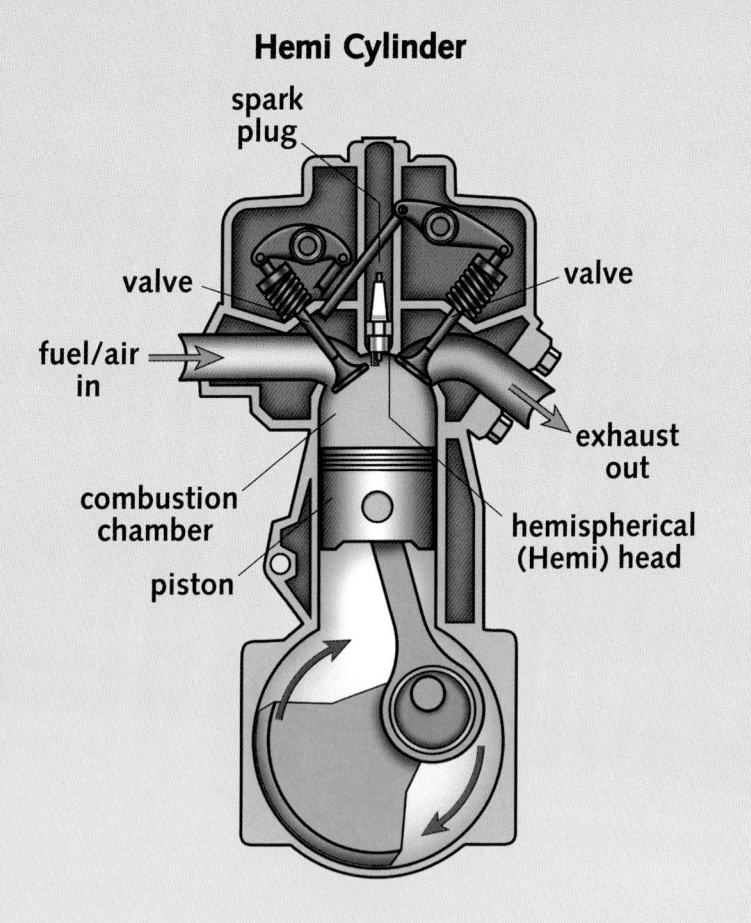

spark plug

valve

valve

fuel/air in

exhaust out

combustion chamber

hemispherical (Hemi) head

piston

A Hemi engine mounted to a dragster

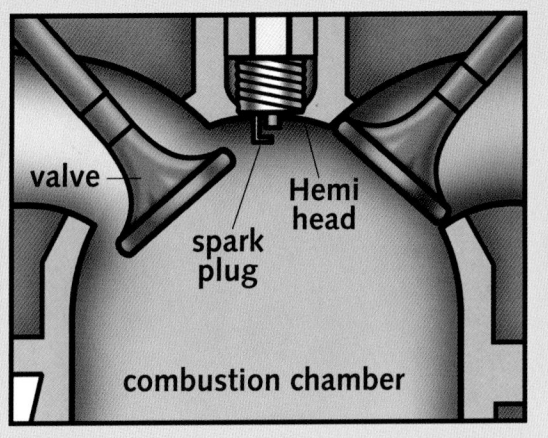

valve

Hemi head

spark plug

combustion chamber

Close-up view of a Hemi's combustion chamber with its rounded (Hemi) top surface.

A Horsepower Stampede

The success of the GTO got other automakers moving. Within months, they were climbing onto the muscle car bandwagon. In early 1964, Oldsmobile launched a special version of its midsized F-85.

Oldsmobile called its first muscle car the 4-4-2.

The following year, Buick introduced the Gran Sport (GS). And Chevrolet rolled out the Chevelle SS 396. This car came with a powerful 396-cubic-inch motor.

Although the first Oldsmobile 4-4-2s came out in 1964, the car continued to be popular among muscle car fans for many years. This is a 1966 version.

By this time, the muscle car race was truly on. Chrysler's first real muscle car was the Dodge Charger. This midsized car showed up for the 1966 model year. It could be purchased with a massive 426 Street Hemi engine that really burned rubber. That same year, Chevrolet introduced a restyled Chevelle SS 396. This hip new machine turned a lot of heads. But it was still a notch below the GTO in popularity. The 1966 Goat turned out to be the best-selling muscle car of all time. Pontiac sold 96,946 for that model year.

Pony Car Power

By 1967 the muscle car era was cruising at full throttle. For that model year, Plymouth introduced the GTX. Its sister company, Dodge, launched the R/T (for road and track). Both machines could be purchased with a massive 440-cubic-inch engine with 375 horsepower that could tear up the streets.

The 1966 Dodge Charger turned heads and blew away the competition with its massive Hemi engine.

Following the huge popularity of the Mustang *(below)*, other companies came out with their own pony cars. The Chevrolet Camaro was one of the most popular. The 1967 Camaro *(left)* sold nearly 200,000 the first year!

Meanwhile, U.S. automakers were eager to take advantage of the Ford Mustang's success. A whole new class of car, the pony car (nicknamed after the Mustang) was taking shape. These cars were small, lightweight, affordable, and very stylish. And they could be purchased with a whole lot of muscle.

For 1967 Chevrolet introduced the Camaro as its pony car. Pontiac came out with the Firebird. Both cars were big hits. American Motors Corporation (AMC)—a small automaker based in Kenosha, Wisconsin—entered the race too. AMC launched a pair of its own pint-sized muscle machines. They were the four-seat Javelin and the two-seat AMX.

Pony cars really caught the attention of the public. Chevrolet sold a staggering 195,765 Camaros for the 1967 model year. And yet, oddly enough, the company that invented the pony car had yet to add actual muscle to its most popular machine. But Ford would jump into the muscle car race in the following year.

The Road Runner *(above)* debuted in 1968. It was named after a speedy cartoon character that outraces and outwits its enemies. Its horn even made the Roadrunner's "Beep-Beep."

Muscle Car Madness

For the 1968 model year, Ford unleashed a new, high-performance engine. The 428-cubic-inch Cobra Jet was available in a bigger and restyled Mustang. The 335-horsepower engine could compete with any car on the road.

That same year saw the appearance of the Plymouth Road Runner. It was one of the fastest and most popular of all the muscle cars. The Road Runner and its sister car, the Dodge Super Bee, were instant hits with the public.

Supercars

The cars described in this book weren't known as muscle cars when they were built. Most people called them supercars. Only after the muscle car era was over did people start calling them muscle cars.

The 1969 Pontiac Firebird Trans Am *(left)* and the 1969 Dodge Daytona *(below)* are two of the rarest muscle cars. Neither car was produced in large numbers.

By 1969 more legendary cars were coming off the assembly line. Ford unveiled the Mustang Mach 1. This was a high-performance package that really roared. That same year, Dodge introduced one of the wildest muscle cars of all time, the original Dodge Daytona. Named after the famous NASCAR speedway, the Daytona was built to race. It had a rounded front end and a high-flying rear spoiler. (This is a wing-shaped part that helps to keep the back end steady at high speeds.) The Daytona had a gigantic 440-cubic-inch engine that produced 375 horsepower.

But perhaps the most famous car to appear in 1969 was the Pontiac Firebird Trans Am. Decked out in racing stripes, stylish wheels, and a rear spoiler, the Trans Am got a lot of attention. At the same time, Pontiac also unleashed a special version of the GTO.

Chevrolet unleashed the powerful Chevelle SS in 1970. Its massive engine gave muscle car fans something to cheer about.

It was known as the Judge. It had a slick design, a shatterproof front bumper, and colorful racing stripes. The Judge was one of the coolest cars on the road.

The muscle car craze reached its peak in 1970. Among the most famous models of that year was the 1970 Chevelle SS. It could be purchased with a massive 454-cubic-inch engine that cranked out an incredible 450 horsepower. Plymouth came out with its own version of the Daytona, the Superbird. The Superbird could reach speeds of up to 200 miles (320 km) per hour.

But the muscle car craze couldn't last forever. So much speed in the hands of young, inexperienced drivers was a dangerous thing.

Too Fast, Too Dirty

During the muscle car era, a lawyer named Ralph Nader had published a powerful book. It was titled *Unsafe at Any Speed*. Nader's book criticized automakers for not making their cars safe enough.

The book caught the attention of the U.S. Congress. All of a sudden, auto safety became a hot issue. So it was only a matter of time before the U.S. government began to frown on muscle cars. After all, who really needed a car that could go 150 or 200 miles (240 or 320 km) per hour?

Dangerous speeds aside, muscle cars became a government target for other reasons. Air pollution was also becoming a major concern. The big, powerful muscle car engines belched out gobs of exhaust fumes. By the early 1970s, Congress had passed antipollution laws that put the brakes on big, muscular engines.

U.S. automakers still produced some great muscle cars in the early 1970s. Buyers could still take home brand-new high-performance Chevelles, Barracudas, Mustangs, Trans Ams, and many other models.

Powerful engines—such as the Hemi in the 1969 Dodge Charger *(top)* and the 1969 Dodge Super Bee's engine *(above)*—produced a lot of speed. But they also sparked criticism about safety. U.S. automakers continued to place high-performance engines in cars, including the 1970 Barracuda engine *(left)*.

Traffic gets backed up on a freeway near Los Angeles, California, in the early 1970s. Tough air pollution laws and high gas prices ended the muscle car era.

But tougher exhaust laws were forcing the buyers to give up a lot of horse-power for the sake of cleaner air.

Muscle car sales dropped off in the early 1970s. Then, in 1973, world events led to a major oil crisis in the United States. Gas prices went through the roof. Automakers focused on building more fuel-efficient cars. Performance—let alone high-perform-ance—was no longer a priority.

By 1974 only one true muscle car was still in production. The 1974 Pontiac Firebird Trans Am could be bought with a massive 455-cubic-inch Super Duty engine. This machine had everything a muscle car fan could want. It had a firebird image on the hood and a sleek look that screamed speed.

Although not everyone realized it at the time, the 1974 Trans Am marked the end of the muscle car era. U.S.

automakers kept producing Trans Ams, Mustangs, Camaros, and other popular sporty cars. But these machines didn't come with the same giant engines of previous years.

Muscle machines have made a comeback in recent years. Some classic muscle cars have been reborn for modern drivers. In 1999 Chrysler launched a new letter series car. These new 300s could be bought with a modern, high-performance Hemi engine. For the 2006 model year, Chrysler unleashed a redesigned Dodge Charger. Chevrolet sells a high-performance SS version of some of its popular cars, like the Monte Carlo and the Cobalt. And speedy versions of Ford's exciting new Mustang have been selling fast. These awesome machines are delivering speed and fun to a whole new generation.

One of the last muscle cars of the era was the 1974 Firebird Trans Am *(above).* In 2006 Dodge reintroduced the popular Charger *(below).*

Chapter Two

MUSCLE CAR CULTURE

The days of the classic muscle car are long gone. But fans of these high-powered machines still enjoy them in many different ways. In the early 2000s, muscle cars are some of the most popular vehicles with car collectors. For these people, the glory days of the muscle car live on at car shows and conventions across the country.

Collecting Muscle Cars

Millions of high-performance cars were built during the muscle car era. Most of these machines have turned to rust. Yet tens of thousands of classic muscle cars are still going strong. Most of them are owned by car collectors.

A car collector might be a very wealthy person who owns dozens of

classic cars. Such people usually have a huge garage for storing their vehicles. Some employ mechanics to keep their cars in top shape.

But most collectors own just one or a few special vehicles. For these people, muscle cars are their favorite hobby.

Some collectors buy cars that are already in great shape. They just want to enjoy looking at and driving these amazing vehicles. But many other collectors buy vehicles that are in bad shape. Then they fix them up. For them, restoring muscle cars is a labor of love.

Customizing Muscle Cars

Customizing a muscle car is fun and creative. The customizer not only fixes

Car collector and pro golfer Bruce Lietzke poses with his car collection. His muscle cars include a 1967 Corvette C2 427 *(bottom left)*, two late 1960s Ford Shelby Mustangs *(upper left, right)*, and a 1960s Plymouth GTX *(upper right)*.

This 1970 Dodge Challenger R/T has been customized for drag racing. A massive supercharger sticks out of the car's hood. The fat rear tires give extra grip to get the car off the starting line in a hurry.

up the car, but he or she adds special parts to make the car unique.

People customize cars in many different ways. For example, a person might cut a hole in the hood to make room for a supercharger. A supercharger, or blower, is a device that sits on top of the engine. It forces air into the engine's cylinders, adding an extra boost of power. And a big, shiny blower also looks really cool sticking out of a car's hood.

Customizers can boost performance in other ways. Adding extrawide tires to the back wheels gives a car more grip. That extra grip helps a car get off the starting line faster in races. And those fat tires look great too. High-performance exhaust pipes called headers add power. They help the engine breathe easier. Adding a bigger carburetor is another popular way to go.

When it comes to customizing a car, chrome tops the list. Chrome engine parts, chrome exhaust pipes, and chrome wheels are the most popular options. Customizers also like to jazz up their cars' interior. They might add fuzzy seats or powerful stereos. Hundreds of companies around the United States make custom parts for all sorts of cars.

Yet by far, the most popular way to customize a muscle car is to give it a fancy paint job. Custom paint jobs include flames, racing stripes, and even illustrations. Custom painting gives a car a unique look.

Restoring Muscle Cars

As time has passed and muscle cars have gotten older, restoring has become more popular. Collectors really value cars that look just like they did when they were first made.

Restoring an old car is hard work and requires attention to detail. The car usually has to be stripped down to the bare body. Then all the paint is removed. Once the paint is gone, the restorer will fix any dents and scratches.

A special paint job sets apart this 1965 Mustang. With its wide rear tires, hood scoop, and roll cage (a structure of bars inside the car to protect the driver in a crash), this 1965 Mustang is ready to race.

The idea is to make the body look as good as new. Once the body is finished, the restorer adds several coats of paint.

When the paint is finished, the restorer begins to put the car back together. He or she might use the car's original parts, or they might buy new ones. Many companies specialize in muscle car parts. Reassembling a car is a big, expensive job.

Once the car is put back together, it's time to take it for a drive. Many restorers show off their cars at local car clubs or at car shows.

Muscle Car Clubs and Shows

The United States is home to hundreds of car clubs. Many of these clubs are made up of muscle car fans. Most clubs have meetings on a regular basis. Many produce newsletters

A restorer carefully puts back the trim after his muscle car has been completely repainted.

A car owner shows off a 1967 Shelby Mustang Fastback GT 350 at a car event in Florida. Shelby Mustangs were specially modified by race car builder Carroll Shelby. Fans can find out about local car shows at http://carshownews.com.

that post upcoming events, including car shows. At the shows, people see and talk about their favorite cars. Some shows feature only muscle cars. Others include all kinds of classic vehicles. Club members share tips for customizing and restoring.

Car shows are usually held in a big place, like a fairground, a big parking lot, or a big auditorium. Car owners line up their cars in rows. They usually open up the hood to show off the engine. Collectors and fans wander around, checking out the cars. Most shows have auctions, where people can buy and sell their cars. Car shows are a fun way to learn about cars and collectors.

Join the Scat Pack Club

During the muscle car era, fans of Dodge cars could join the Scat Pack Club. For a small membership fee, Scat Packers received a pack of cool decals, patches *(right)*, and a T-shirt featuring images of Dodge's high-performance cars.

Races and Cruises

You'd be wrong if you thought muscle cars just sit still at shows. Many car events feature races and cruises too.

Muscle cars were built to go fast—faster than the speed limit. But driving over the speed limit is illegal. So many car shows include races. The races take place on tracks where drivers can go full throttle without getting the cops on their tail.

Drag racing is the most popular kind of racing. In a drag race, two cars compete on a short, straight track—usually a quarter-mile track. Straight-line speed is the goal of drag racing. The car that covers the distance in the shortest amount of time is the winner.

Drag racing is fun to watch. The smell of burning rubber, the roar of engines, and the screaming crowds are really exciting. And drag racing is

A 1968 Plymouth GTX screeches down the track at a car show drag race in Pomona, California.

The owner of a 1968 Shelby Mustang shows off his engine during cruising night in Somerville, New Jersey.

pretty safe too. Since the cars just drive straight for a short distance, crashes are rare.

Cruising is another fun car activity. Most car conventions feature cruises. These events usually take place in the evening, after the main part of the show has ended. Owners drive down a street or highway, forming a long line of classic cars. Spectators stop along the side of the road to watch these amazing cars roll past.

Collectibles and Modeling

Not everyone can afford to own a real muscle car. And not everyone has the skills needed to fix up one of these classic machines. You may not even be old enough to drive, let alone own a car! But there are lots of ways to enjoy muscle cars without actually owning the real thing.

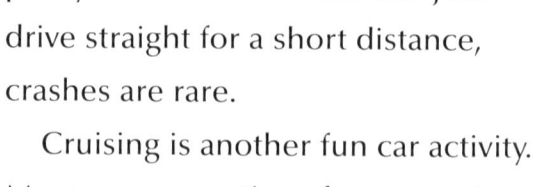

Hot Wheels and Matchbox Collectibles

Hot Wheels and Matchbox miniature die-cast cars have been popular collector's items for many years. In the 1960s and 1970s, the makers of Hot Wheels and Matchbox cars produced small copies of many popular muscle car models. And they continue to make them, including this modified 1969 Dodge Charger Daytona (right).

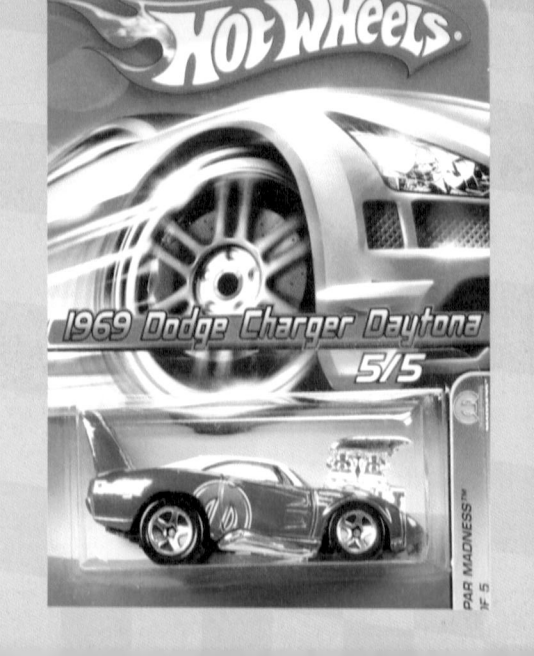

Revell is just one of the companies that make plastic models of muscle cars.

Modelers can assemble scale models of their favorite cars and paint them any color they want. A skilled painter can even add flames, illustrations, and custom racing stripes.

Muscle Car Media

Real muscle car fans just can't get enough of their favorite vehicles. They read muscle car magazines, such as *Musclecar Enthusiast, Muscle Car Review,* and *Hemmings Muscle Machines.* These magazines feature articles on old and new muscle cars. They also have interviews with collectors and reviews of car shows and auctions.

One way is by purchasing collectibles. Muscle car collectibles include die-cast metal cars. Companies such as Ertl, GMP, and ExactDetail make dozens of die-cast metal model cars, including many muscle car replicas. These models are not life size. But they are designed to look as realistic as possible.

Another popular way to enjoy muscle cars is by building models of them. Companies like Revell, AMT, and Ertl make excellent plastic model kits.

TV networks—such as MTV, Speed Channel, and the Learning Channel (TLC)—run shows about cars. Speed Channel's *American Muscle Car* explores the history of these awesome machines. Each half-hour episode covers the history of a particular model, like the Pontiac GTO or the Plymouth Barracuda.

Muscle Cars in Movies and on TV

During the late 1960s and early 1970s, Hollywood filmmakers made a number of popular movies that featured muscle cars. The best-known muscle car movie is *Bullitt* (1968), starring Steve McQueen. McQueen plays Frank Bullitt, a San Francisco cop.

Bullitt features one of the most famous car chase scenes in movie history. Driving a high-performance Ford Mustang GT, McQueen races through the hilly streets of San Francisco. He is chasing a pair of bad guys in a Dodge Charger.

The Dukes of Hazzard was a popular TV show of the 1980s. It featured an orange 1969 Dodge Charger *(above right)*. The fun and exciting show featured lots of car chases—and car crashes. More than 200 Dodge Chargers were destroyed during the show's seven-year run.

Most other car shows feature makeovers, where mechanics take old cars and customize them in crazy ways. For example, MTV's popular show *Pimp My Ride*, takes old, beat-up cars and turns them into incredible custom machines. *Overhaulin'*, on the TLC network, does the same thing. What makes *Overhaulin'* fun is that the owner doesn't know his or her car is being redone. People are pretty excited when they see what happens to their old heaps!

The Dukes' 1969 Dodge Charger

Auto design wizard Chip Foose puts finishing touches on an *Overhaulin'* project.

Muscle Car Restoration

In the early 2000s, Mike and June Key decided to restore a 1966 Ford Mustang. The heap was in a bad state. It was rusted throughout, and the interior was In ruins.

Mike and June stripped the car themselves. What was left was just the chassis and the front and rear suspension. Their next step was to scrape and weld the car's underside and the area where a new engine would go. Mike replaced the dash and other worn-out parts. He then painted all these parts Satin Black. The couple got help from some expert friends. One fixed the badly rusted metal parts of the car's exterior. Another primed and painted the exterior bright red.

June got back into the act when the windows, doors, and carpets were installed. Together, she and Mike struggled through the job of recovering the front and back seats, also in bright red.

By 2005 the car was ready for driving. Mike says it's very close to how the car came out of the factory in 1966. Sweet!

1. The rusted-out 1966 Ford Mustang arrived at the house of Mike and June Key. Their first idea was to restore the car so it could be just an additional vehicle for the family, not a show car. But after they got going on the restoration, they realized that, no matter what, the project would be a lot of work. They decided to restore the car to its original look.

2. Preparing the car's body for painting took a huge amount of time. Mike's friend Paul Wayling (below) scraped and sanded the larger sections of the metal exterior that had been bent or badly rusted. Mike helped by taking care of smaller dings.

3. A crack in the chassis meant the area needed to be cleaned up and sanded before welding could take place.

4. Mike completely cleaned out and repainted the engine bay. A beautiful cleaned-up engine was ready to put inside.

5. A special room was needed to completely spray the body with its new bright red color.

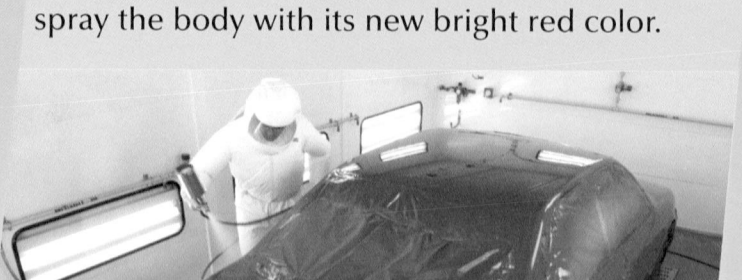

6. June Key worked hard to get the upholstery just right on the bucket seats *(inset)*. Two years after they started, the Keys had a fully restored and fun-to-drive Mustang.

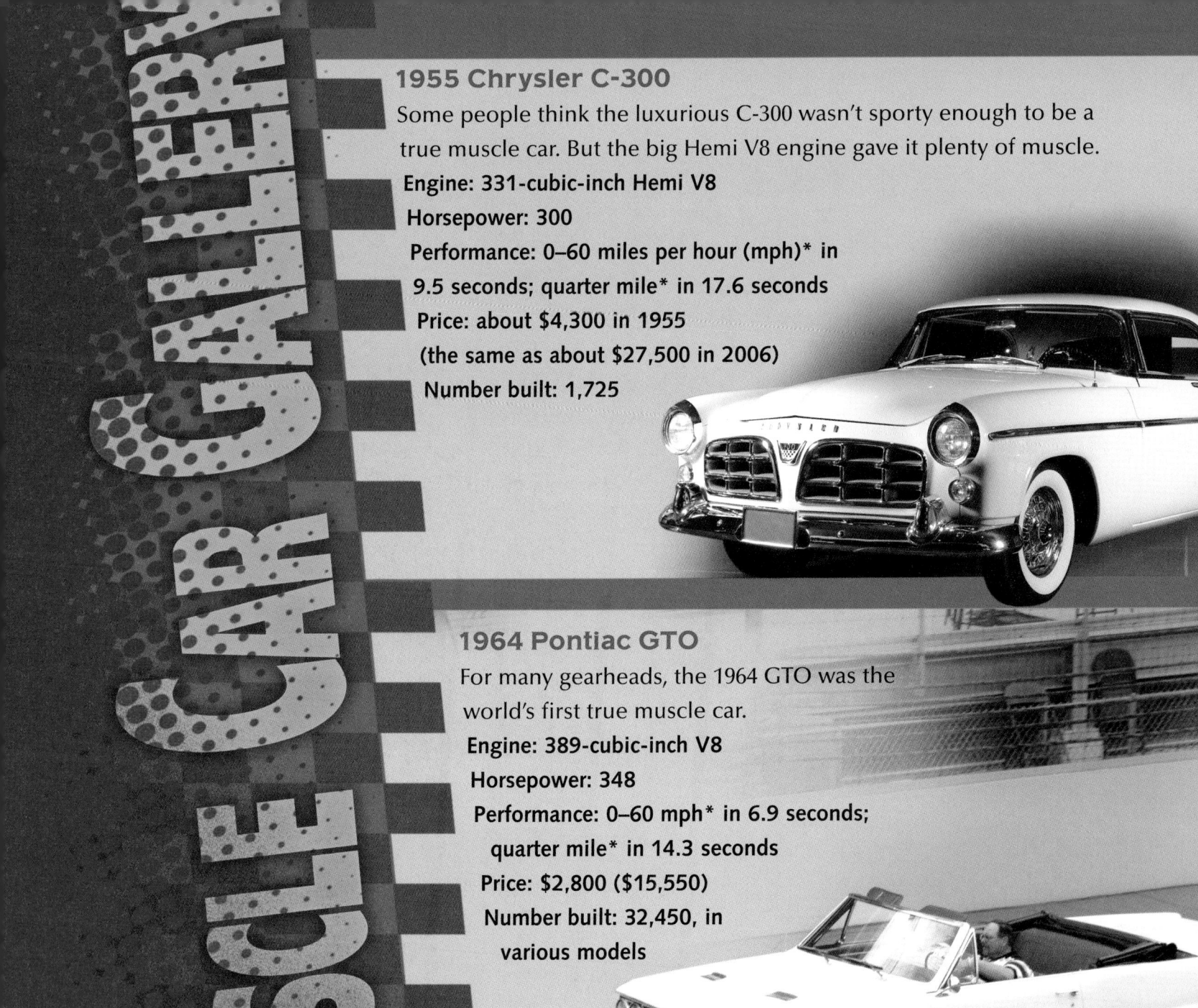

1955 Chrysler C-300

Some people think the luxurious C-300 wasn't sporty enough to be a true muscle car. But the big Hemi V8 engine gave it plenty of muscle.

Engine: 331-cubic-inch Hemi V8

Horsepower: 300

Performance: 0–60 miles per hour (mph)* in 9.5 seconds; quarter mile* in 17.6 seconds

Price: about $4,300 in 1955 (the same as about $27,500 in 2006)

Number built: 1,725

1964 Pontiac GTO

For many gearheads, the 1964 GTO was the world's first true muscle car.

Engine: 389-cubic-inch V8

Horsepower: 348

Performance: 0–60 mph* in 6.9 seconds; quarter mile* in 14.3 seconds

Price: $2,800 ($15,550)

Number built: 32,450, in various models

* 0–97 kmph; 0.40 km

1966 Oldsmobile 4-4-2

Oldsmobile called its most famous muscle car the 4-4-2. The numbers stand for a four-barrel carburetor, a four-on-the-floor (four-speed shifter mounted on the floor) transmission, and dual exhausts.

Engine: 400-cubic-inch V8

Horsepower: 350

Performance: 0–60 mph* in 7.1 seconds; quarter mile* in 15.5 seconds

Price: $4,300 ($22,870)

Number built: 21,997 in various models

1967 Chevrolet Corvette Sting Ray L-88

Some car fans don't count the Corvette as a true muscle car. But the legendary and rare L-88 Corvette had as much muscle as any car built during the muscle car era.

Engine: 427-cubic-inch L-88 V8

Horsepower: 430

Performance: 0–60 mph* in 5.5 seconds; quarter mile* in 13.8 seconds

Price: $5,675 ($29,250)

Number built: 20

1967 Chevrolet Camaro Z/28

The Z/28 was originally created to compete against Mustangs in races. To qualify the car for racing, Chevrolet had to make the car available to the public. For the next few years, Camaros were best on the track and had caught on with the pony car crowd.

Engine: 302-cubic-inch V8

Horsepower: 290

Performance: 0–60 mph* in 7.4 seconds; quarter mile* in 14.9 seconds

Price: $3,380 ($17,425)

Number built: 602

1968 Dodge Charger R/T

Car review magazines used words like *brute, mean,* and *nasty* to describe the Charger.

Engine: 440-cubic-inch Magnum V8

Horsepower: 375

Performance: 0–60 mph* in 6.0 seconds; quarter mile* in 13.5 seconds

Price: $4,190 ($20,750)

Number built: 59

* 0–97 kmph; 0.40 km

1968 Ford Cobra Jet Mustang

Ford was the last automaker to jump onto the muscle car bandwagon. But the 1968 Cobra Jet Mustang had the power to make up for lost time.

Engine: 428-cubic-inch Cobra Jet V8

Horsepower: 335

Performance: 0–60 mph* in 6.9 seconds; quarter mile* in 13.6 seconds

Price: $3,600 ($17,800)

Number built: 2,287

1968 Plymouth Road Runner

Plymouth built the Road Runner to make it affordable to young drivers. The car didn't even have carpet inside. But for an extra $714 ($3,500), the buyer could request a 426-cubic-inch Hemi engine that produced a whopping 425 horsepower.

Engine: 426-cubic-inch Hemi V8

Horsepower: 425

Performance: 0–60 mph* in 5.3 seconds; quarter mile* in about 13 seconds

Price: $3,034 ($15,000)

Number built: 840

1969 Pontiac Firebird Trans Am

The Trans Am was the only muscle car that made it from the 1960s to the 1990s. In fact, GM celebrated the car's 30th birthday with a special blue and white model that cost about $35,000.

Engine: 400-cubic-inch V8

Horsepower: 355

Performance: 0–60 mph* unknown;
  quarter mile* In 14.1 seconds

Price: $3,890 ($18,265)

Number built: 689

1970 American Motors AMX

American Motors was slow to join the muscle car race. Not until 1968 did AMC introduce its own high-performance machine, the two-seat AMX. The little muscle car had plenty of power, though. The 1970 version was available with a 390-cubic-inch V8 that produced 325 horsepower.

Engine: 390-cubic-inch V8

Horsepower: 325

Performance: 0–60 mph* in
  6.6 seconds;
    quarter mile* in 14.7 seconds

Price: $3,560 ($15,800)

Number built: 4,116

40

* 0–97 kmph; 0.40 km

1970 Buick GSX

Some people saw Buick's first Gran Sport (GS) as hot rods for older buyers. But by 1970, when Buick came out with the GSX, that car had evolved to appeal to a younger crowd too. It came in only two colors—Saturn Yellow and Apollo White.

Engine: 455-cubic-inch V8

Horsepower: 360

Performance: 0–60 mph* in 6.2 seconds; quarter mile* in 14.0 seconds

Price: $4,479 ($19,900)

Number built: 400

1970 Chevrolet Chevelle SS

The Chevelle SS LS-6 454 was Chevrolet's most muscular car ever, generating at least 450 horsepower. Available with racing stripes, this car screamed performance. The 1970 Chevelle SS is one of the most popular collector cars.

Engine: 454-cubic-inch V8

Horsepower: 450

Performance: 0–60 mph* in 5.4 seconds; quarter mile* in 13.2 seconds

Price: $4,475 ($19,900)

Number built: 3,773

1970 Mercury Cougar Eliminator

By 1970 the Mercury Cougar could be purchased with a 428 cubic-inch Cobra Jet V8. The Eliminator eliminated much of the competition at drag races around the country.

Engine: 428-cubic-inch Cobra Jet V8

Horsepower: 335

Performance: 0–60 mph in 7.6 seconds; quarter mile in 14.4 seconds

Price: $3,200 ($14,250)

Number built: 2,200 (including all engine options)

1970 Plymouth Superbird

With a rounded nose and a tall rear spoiler (nicknamed a towel rack), the Superbird was built for racing. On the track, it blew away the NASCAR competition.

Engine: 426-cubic-inch Hemi V8

Horsepower: 425

Performance: 0–60* mph in 5.9 seconds; quarter mile* in 14.3   seconds

Price: $4,298 ($19,100)

Number built: 135

* 0–97 kmph; 0.40 km

1970 Pontiac GTO Judge

Hip decals and colorful body stripes set apart the Judge from Pontiac's other GTOs. Legend has it that the car was named after a skit from the hit comedy show *Laugh-In*.

Engine: 400-cubic-inch V8

Horsepower: 366

Performance: 0–60 mph* in 6.6 seconds; quarter mile* in 14.6 seconds

Price: $3,600 ($16,000)

Number built: 3,797, in various models

1971 Ford Mustang Mach 1

By 1971 the Mustang had grown quite a bit in size and weight, and performance suffered. Ford offered two high-performance Mustangs for 1971—the Boss 351 and the Mach 1 *(right)*. The Mach 1's dramatic styling was highly praised.

Engine: 351-cubic-inch V8

Horsepower: 330

Performance: 0–60 mph* in 5.9 seconds; quarter-mile* in 14.1 seconds

Price: $4,817 ($17,550)

Number built: 36,499

1974 Pontiac Firebird Trans Am 455 Super Duty

The 1974 Trans Am 455 Super Duty was the last great muscle car of the muscle car era. Pontiac's engineers had to do a lot of work on the engine to allow it to pass government air pollution tests. But the car still delivered plenty of horsepower.

Engine: 455-cubic-inch Super Duty V8

Horsepower: 290

Performance: 0–60 mph* in 5.9 seconds; quarter mile* in 14.3 seconds

Price: $4,350 ($15,200)

Number built: 943

2003 Ford Mustang Mach 1

For the 2003 model year, Ford brought back the Mach 1 Mustang. Customers could choose from a number of colors, such as Torch Red and Zinc Yellow. Black racing stripes and a shaker hood scoop completed the powerful package.

Engine: 4.6-liter V8

Horsepower: 305

Performance: 0–60 mph* in 5.3 seconds; quarter mile* in 13.8 seconds

Price: $28,995

Number built: 9,652

* 0–97 kmph; 0.40 km

2004 Pontiac GTO

After a 30-year absence, Pontiac brought back the GTO for 2004. The sporty two-door coupe features leather seats and a stylish interior. It also comes with a muscular engine that's built for speed.

Engine: 5.7-liter V8

Horsepower: 350

Performance: 0–60 mph* in 5.3 seconds; quarter mile* in 13.6 seconds

Price: $33,000

Number built: 18,000

2006 Dodge Charger R/T

One of the most popular muscle cars of all time muscled its way back into auto headlines at the 2005 North American International Auto Show in Detroit. The stylish newcomer sports power, with a Hemi option, as well as every-day riding efficiency.

Engine: 5.7 liter Hemi V8

Horsepower: 340

Performance: 0–60 mph* in 6.2 seconds; quarter mile* in 14.3 seconds

Price: $30,395

Number built: in production as of 2006

Glossary

acceleration: a vehicle's ability to gain speed within a short time

combustion chamber: the space inside an engine where combustion (burning) takes place

cylinder: a tube-shaped chamber in an engine

front spoiler: a device that is placed on the front of a car, usually below the bumper, that helps a car grip the road. A front spoiler redirects air coming toward the front of the car. It presses the front of the car downward, helping the car to grip the road at high speed.

header: a high-performance exhaust pipe. Headers are designed to add horsepower by helping the engine breathe as efficiently as possible.

high-performance: something that performs well at high speeds

hood scoop: a slot or hole in a car's hood that allows extra air to reach the carburetor. Hood scoops improve an engine's horsepower.

horsepower: as a car term, a unit used to measure the amount of power an engine can produce. Horsepower was originally measured as the amount of work a certain kind of horse could do in a minute.

model: the specific design of a car or other product

model year: the particular year that a car is made. For U.S. automakers, the model year begins a few months earlier than the calendar year. For example, cars for the 1968 model year were available in late 1967.

rear spoiler: a wing-shaped device that is attached to the rear of a car. When air moves past the spoiler at high speed, the spoiler pushes the rear end of the car downward, helping to keep the rear stable.

supercharger: a device on the top of an engine that forces air into the combustion chambers, creating more horsepower

Selected Bibliography

Auto Editors of Consumer Guide. *Muscle Car Chronicle*. Lincolnwood, IL: Publications International, 2003.

Benson, Michael. *Muscle Cars: Thunder and Greased Lightning*. New York: Todtri Book Publishers, 1996.

Campisano, Jim. *American Muscle Cars*. New York: Barnes and Noble Books, 1999.

Georgano, Nick. *The American Automobile: A Century, 1893–1993*. New York: Smithmark Publishers, 1992.

Leffingwell, Randy. *American Muscle: Muscle Cars from the Otis Chandler Collection*. Osceola, WI: MBI Publishing Company, 1990.

Mueller, Mike. *Essential Musclecars*. Saint Paul: Motorbooks International, 2004.

____. *Motor City Muscle*. Osceola, WI: MBI Publishing Company, 1997.

____. *Muscle Car Icons: Ford, Chevy & Chrysler*. Saint Paul: Crestline, 2003.

Further Reading

Braun, Eric. *Hot Rods*. Minneapolis: Lerner Publications Company, 2007.

Doeden, Matt. *Stock Cars*. Minneapolis: Lerner Publications Company, 2007.

Johnstone, Mike. *NASCAR*. Minneapolis: LernerSports, 2002.

LaFontaine, Bruce. *American Muscle Cars: 1960–1975*. Mineola, NY: Dover Publications, 2001.

Mueller, Mike. *The Corvette*. Saint Paul: Crestline, 2003.

Newhardt, David. *The Mustang*. Saint Paul: Crestline, 2003.

Nicholls, Richard. *American Classic Cars*. New York: Barnes and Noble Books, 2002.

Piehl, Janet. *Formula One Race Cars*. Minneapolis: Lerner Publications Company, 2007.

Willson, Quentin. *Classic American Cars*. New York: Dorling Kindersley, 1997.

____. *Great Car*. New York: Dorling Kindersley, 2001.

Websites

Hemmings Motor News
   http://www.hemmings.com
   Hemmings Motor News is a top resource for any muscle car fan. The company publishes several popular magazines, including *Hemmings Muscle Machines, Hemmings Motor News,* and *Hemmings Classic Cars.* The company's website features names and addresses of auto clubs and much, much more.

Musclecarclub.com
   http://www.musclecarclub.com/main.shtml
   The official website of the Muscle Car Club in the United States has informative and photo-filled articles on virtually every muscle car model ever built.

Musclecarplanet.com
   http://www.musclecarplanet.com
   This site includes articles and interesting facts about muscle cars and information on muscle car shows and clubs around the country.

Muscle Cars.net
   http://musclecars.net
   This site features photos of all of the most popular classic muscle cars, as well as information about upcoming muscle car cruises.

Index

About the Author

Jeffrey Zuehlke is a writer and editor who lives in Minneapolis. He has written more than a dozen nonfiction books for children. His dream muscle car is a 1970 Chevrolet Chevelle SS 454.

About the Consultant

Jan Lahtonen is a safety engineer, auto mechanic, and lifelong car fan. He has raced sports cars, worked as a performance driving instructor, and is a member of the Porsche Club of America and the Audi Club of America. He has owned several muscle cars, including a 1964 Pontiac GTO, a 1965 Chevy Impala SS 409, and 1969 Dodge Charger R/T.

Photo Acknowledgments

The images in this book are used with the permission of: © Mike Key, pp. 4–5, 6, 16, 17 (both), 19 (bottom), 20, 21 (all), 24 (background), 26, 27, 28, 29 (top), 34 (both), 35 (top, right, bottom), 38 (bottom), 39 (top), 41 (bottom), 42 (bottom), 43 (bottom); Library of Congress, pp. 6 (background), 7 (LC-USZ62-92268); www.ronkimballstock.com, p. 9; © Laura Westlund/Independent Picture Service, pp. 10, 14 (diagrams); Neill Bruce/www.brucephoto.co.uk, p. 11; © Ralph Crane/Time Life Pictures/Getty Images, p. 12; © Jerry Heasley, pp. 13, 15, 18, 19 (top), 37 (both), 38 (top), 39 (bottom), 40 (both), 41 (top), 42 (top), 43 (top); © PhotoEquity/Artemis Images, p. 14; © Bettmann/CORBIS, p. 22; Copyright 2006 GM Corp. Used with permission, GM Media Archive, pp. 23 (top), 44 (top); © Henny Ray Abrams/Reuters/CORBIS, p. 23 (bottom); © Ronald Martinez/Allsport/Getty Images, p. 25; © Todd Strand/Independent Picture Service, pp. 29 (bottom), 32, 45 (top); © Mirek Towski/Time Life Pictures/Getty Images, p. 30; AP/Wide World Photos, pp. 31 (top), 33 (bottom); © Erica Johnson/Independent Picture Service, p. 31 (bottom); © Frazer Harrison/Getty Images, p. 33 (top); © Roger Ball/CORBIS, p. 35 (left); Courtesy of the Petersen Automotive Museum, "Musclecars: Power to the People!" exhibition, Collection of Bill Madden, p. 36 (top); © Indy GTO Association/Artemis Images, p. 36 (bottom); Ford Motor Company, p. 44 (bottom); © STAN HONDA/AFP/Getty Images, p. 45 (bottom).

Front Cover: © Mike Key.